For my parents

Anyone who tries to penetrate
the past with the knife of the
present will always act in vain.
The past is invulnerable.
Such attempts can only cause
the present or the future to bleed.

—Gregor Brand

THE OTHER SIDE OF THE WALL

SIMON SCHWARTZ

TRANSLATED BY LAURA WATKINSON

GRAPHIC UNIVERSE™ • MINNEAPOLIS

Story and art by Simon Schwartz
Translation by Laura Watkinson

First American edition published in 2015 by Graphic Universe™.
Published by arrangement with Avant-Verlag.

drüben! by Simon Schwartz
Copyright © Simon Schwartz & Avant-Verlag 2009. Rights arranged through Nicolas Grivel Agency.

English translation copyright © 2015 by Laura Watkinson

Graphic Universe™ is a trademark of Lerner Publishing Group, Inc.

Graphic Universe™
A division of Lerner Publishing Group, Inc.
241 First Avenue North
Minneapolis, MN 55401 USA

For reading levels and more information, look up this title at www.lernerbooks.com.

Main body text set in King George Bold Clean 9.5/9.5. Typeface provided by Chank.

The Cataloging-in-Publication Data for *The Other Side of the Wall* is on file at the Library of Congress.
ISBN: 978-1-4677-5840-6 (lib. bdg. : alk. paper)
ISBN: 978-1-4677-6028-7 (pbk.)
ISBN: 978-1-4677-7839-8 (EB pdf)

Manufactured in the United States of America
1 – DP – 12/31/14

My parents met in Erfurt in 1974.

They were both studying to be teachers of art and math.

After the man was gone, my dad found that he was holding his first-ever twenty Deutsche Mark bill.

We lived with two of my parents' university friends at first.

They'd left the DDR more than a year earlier. We shared the apartment with three other families. All of the residents were people who had "skipped out on" the DDR.

Skipping out on the country—I've never liked that idea. East Germans used it to insult anyone who had left the DDR. As if they were dodging something or shirking their responsibility.

When we arrived in West Berlin in 1984, we had no money and nowhere to live. Just the things in our suitcases and the clothes on our backs.

West Berlin was such a contrast. People could tell right away that we were from the East—because of our clothes, the way we spoke, and our obvious lack of confidence.

But everyone was friendly toward us.

It was the spring of 1987, and we were living in a beautiful old apartment just a few steps away from the Berlin Wall.

My dad wrote to tell them about our new life.

A few days later, the letter was returned with a brief handwritten note.

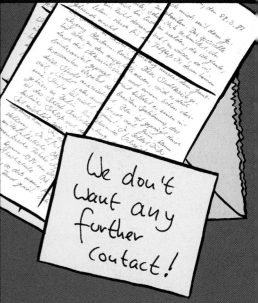

We don't want any further contact!

Three years after leaving the DDR* with me and my mom, my dad wrote his parents a letter.

They were still living in the DDR.

We were living in West Berlin. My dad hadn't seen or spoken to his parents since we'd left.

I was four years old at the time and going to kindergarten in the Kreuzberg neighborhood.

*Deutsche Demokratische Republik, or German Democratic Republic

My dad came from a model socialist family. Like his parents, he was a member of the SED*. His father was the manager of a print shop, and his mother was also a dedicated supporter of the DDR.

Even before the war, my grandmother's parents had encouraged her interest in communism. Along with her father, she became a member of the KPD**.

She met my grandfather at a party meeting after the war.

My grandfather came from a Jewish background. The Nazis had sent many of his family members to the death camps. But he'd been able to go into hiding, so he avoided capture.

*Sozialistische Einheitspartei Deutschlands, or Socialist Unity Party of Germany
**Kommunistische Partei Deutschlands, or Communist Party of Germany
***May 1. Day of Action against War, Fascism, and Hunger

The horrors of dictatorship and the war had left a deep impression on them. Driven by their wish for no more war, no more uniforms, they enthusiastically helped construct the new state.

My dad loved his parents and automatically adopted their view of the world.

Hurry. Or you're going to be late.

All right, Mom.

He liked going to school and enjoyed being a member of the Pioneers, a communist group for children.

Good morning, Frau Reidel!

Ah, there you are.

My mom's childhood was different, though. Her parents didn't fully reject the DDR, but they had lots of contacts in the West.

In the days before the Wall, my mom's uncle had fled to the West. Before my mom was born, her parents had thought about following him.

Her cousin from the West, who was the same age as her, often came to visit, and he told her all about his life.

As a teenager, my mom longed to see that strange, forbidden world and to maybe marry Mick Jagger one day.

Even though *Bravo* magazine made the West sound very tempting, my mom didn't yet have any doubts about the "victory of socialism."

My dad had heard of the Rolling Stones too, but he didn't listen to their music. He had no contacts in the West, so he didn't own any of their records.

At high school, he was an active member of the Free German Youth and he noticed that his fellow students were sometimes a bit chilly toward him.

Hey, are you coming to Frank's after school?

His aunt in the West gave him a Jimi Hendrix album. We're all going to tape it.

Jürgen and Karl are coming too.

A pop music magazine from West Germany, secretly smuggled into East Germany

Hey, what are you guys doing later?

Um, homework.

Got visitors coming.

My mom and her girlfriends went to almost every dance in the Dresden area.

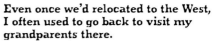

Even once we'd relocated to the West, I often used to go back to visit my grandparents there.

My mom always took me to the border crossing point at Bahnhof Friedrichstraße.

A coworker of my mom's usually accompanied me across the border.

Make sure you hold onto her hand, okay? And give Grandma and Grandpa my love.

Unlike my parents, I was permitted to return to the DDR.

I love you.

But there was always that worry that I wouldn't be allowed back home.

And then we'd go straight to Dresden.

Those vacations with my grandparents were always great. Everyone was happy to see me.

We went on a steamer on the River Elbe . . .

... visited the Sächsische Schweiz district and saw a Winnetou adventure at the Rathen open-air theater ...

... and went to the Kleinwelka dinosaur park.

As a child, I hardly noticed the differences from my life in West Berlin.

Grandma, are you sure this is a vegetable store?

The time always flew by. I never felt homesick.

I never visited my dad's parents in Zwickau, though.

For a long time, I thought it was completely normal to have just one set of grandparents: a grandma and grandpa I hardly ever saw and never saw without stepping over hurdles.

I realized at a young age that not everyone was as free to move around as me.

And why does everyone at kindergarten have two grandmas and grandpas except me?

Unlike my mom, my dad was kind of reluctant when he started his studies.

He actually wanted to study art, but there was a shortage of teachers in the DDR, so he'd been persuaded to train as an art and math teacher.

But of course, no one told him that the DDR rarely permitted a second round of studies.

Look, there's some painting involved, and you can always study art later.

$f(x) = e^x$
$f'(x) = 2e^{2x}$
$F(x) =$

$f(x) = e^{2x}$
$f'(x) = 2e^{2x}$
$F(x) = \frac{1}{2}e^{2x}$

The group of students in my mom and dad's courses soon became a tight-knit community.

My parents' time at university was pretty carefree.

What's up with those two?

What do you think?!

You're in the church?

You're in the party?

Military training was compulsory for all students.

And students became more and more aware of the contradictions between propaganda and the real world.

Hey! Did you all hear about the guy in the other class who got thrown out?

You mean the one who suggested a few improvements to socialism in the student paper?

But he's in the party, isn't he?

Yeah! And his girlfriend made a petition for him and sent it to the minister of education. Well, now they've thrown out the girl and everyone who signed.

Even my dad started to have doubts.

But his girlfriend's in the party too. And didn't the FDJ actually call upon people to think about improvements? I don't understand.

*Manfred Krug is a well-known German actor and singer. After his friend Wolf Biermann was expatriated, Krug also left the DDR.
**Wolf Biermann is a popular German singer-songwriter. Biermann was forced to leave the DDR after writing songs that criticized its institutions.

In twenty minutes, we will arrive at Zwickau.

My dad felt increasingly uncomfortable in his parents' world. He was in his early twenties, but he still hadn't quite cut the umbilical cord.

It seemed impossible to combine the two worlds he lived in.

After graduation, my dad took over a ninth-grade class at a high school.

Okay, and be sure to remind your moms and dads that it's parents' night tomorrow.

Riiinngg

Michi, you spaz! Out of the way! Heh-heh.

Oww!

*Erich Honecker

Hey! Thank goodness you're here!

You've had a break-in. Your wife's upstairs and she's really upset.

His girlfriend wasn't worried at first. Sometimes he'd go away for a few days.

But yesterday, the Stasi* turned her entire apartment upside down. That's when she found out.

But why?

He applied for an exit permit. I guess he indicated that his sister in the West would try to help him from her side. So they accused him of illegal contact with Western authorities.

There's something else we need to tell you.

*DDR state security service

We've applied for an exit permit too.

After a large number of well-known individuals left the country, as a reaction to the denaturalization of singer-songwriter Wolf Biermann, the general public became increasingly aware that they could—legally—leave the DDR.

Wolf Biermann

Manfred Krug

Nina Hagen

This had been formalized in the 1975 Helsinki Accords, an effort to improve relations between communist states and the West.

b. Fed. Allemagne

Re. Allen

As mentioned, my dad had a teaching job at the University of Erfurt by then.

Comrade Schwartz, could I speak to you for a moment, please?

Of course.

As you know, the fourth-semester students are going to military camp next week. As part of the program for those students who are not participating, you are to give a lecture.

Your theme is "The Just War and the Unjust War." Tuesday at eleven in the main auditorium.

That same day, my parents applied for permanent emigration from the DDR.

The reason they gave was a wish to be reunited with my mom's relatives in the West.

A few days later, my dad was told to report to the university's main auditorium.

In front of the entire teaching staff and party leaders, he was thrown out of the party and removed from his position at the university.

The whole process took several hours.

My dad didn't say a word.

After that, my dad's former students crossed the street when they saw him.

My mom and dad met up with my dad's parents to tell them about their decision.

It's still hard for me to understand exactly what happened that day.

The news must have been a shock for my grandparents. Inconceivable. Their own son was a stranger to them.

My dad had always kept his dissatisfaction a secret from his parents. Maybe he knew they wouldn't understand.

Soon after that, my grandparents made it clear that further contact was out of the question until my dad withdrew his application to leave the DDR.

For years, I found it impossible to understand how anyone could reject their own child like that, but of course that's only half of the truth.

My grandparents must have felt just as rejected by their son. They didn't realize that my parents' decision was not a reaction against them but against the system.

But once again, my dad was unable to explain himself. He stonewalled them.

I suspect that both sides had never really talked to each other enough.

Next, my mom and dad drove on to visit my mom's parents.

It didn't come as a huge surprise to them.

We understand. If we were younger, we'd probably make the same decision ourselves.

They cried all evening.

I have no idea what my dad's parents did.

Shortly after that, I was born.

My dad's parents sent us a letter and a package.

The package contained a book of fairy tales and a really impersonal dedication.

The letter was for my parents. It was full of bitterness and accusations.

I didn't meet my dad's parents until 1990, after the Wall came down. We went to visit them in Zwickau.

It was the first time my parents had seen them since they'd informed them of their plans to leave the DDR nine years before.

Normally we listened to music or sang on the Autobahn. Not that time.

I can't say I was very eager to meet my "new" grandparents. I actually felt like the whole business had nothing to do with me.

I have no idea what was going through my parents' minds, but I felt very strange.

I can't remember why I was the first to speak. Perhaps I understood subconsciously that it was my job to break the ice.

Coffee and cake were served.

They gave me lots of big, heavy books.

The conversation didn't exactly flow.

I didn't understand most of what they talked about.

I just remember feeling incredibly out of my element.

We had to wait three years for our exit permit to be granted. The authorities in Erfurt were still frozen in a Stalinist ice age.

My mom had started working as a restorer for the church—the unofficial opposition.

Meanwhile, my dad stayed at home and looked after me. Because of our application to leave the DDR, he couldn't get work.

Police!
Open the door!

Boom
Boom

Herr Schwartz. Criminal investigation department. Come with us!

Sit down!

Where were you on March 25, 1983, around 2:30 p.m.?

Um, that was last Friday, right? I was at home as usual, looking after my son.

Such unwarranted interrogations happened again and again. Whenever someone committed a crime against the state, like tearing down a flag, my dad was automatically considered a suspect.

My parents tried to keep a very low profile, because the authorities were obviously looking for something to use against them. Even an unstamped tram ticket would have been enough.

Excuse me, could I have a quick word?

The Stasi came to see me today. They asked me about you. I told them you were very quiet and friendly neighbors.

What on Earth have you done?

In a repressive system, the value of true and loyal friends cannot be overestimated.

They supported one another and were able to speak freely—to share their concerns about the decision they'd made.

Our exit permit has been approved. We're leaving for West Berlin tomorrow.

My parents were among the first East Germans to apply for permanent emigration, and many of their friends submitted applications too.

Gradually, the others all left the country. We were the only ones who still were not permitted to leave. My parents were completely isolated.

Over the years, the Stasi constantly spied on my parents and harassed them, sometimes in broad daylight.

Heh-heh.

My parents didn't find out about the other actions planned against them, even plans for arrest, until after the Wall fell—when they got to look at their files.

But even before the Wall came down, they had their suspicions.

Although my mom and dad didn't openly protest, their clothes and appearance clearly showed they were outsiders and didn't belong to the system.

Short on cash, they started to sell off the contents of our house, including rare books and prints.

A foreign journalist who was a friend of my parents took some of my dad's pictures to West Berlin. It cost a fortune to export your own art, as it was considered the property of the DDR.

During those years of waiting, my dad ran to the mailbox every morning, hoping that the exit permit had arrived. Every time, he was disappointed.

We were living out of boxes.

But one day . . .
Boom
Boom
Your departure has been set for today. Report to City Hall at twelve.
My parents had received and completed the paperwork a week before.
Here are your denaturalization documents and identity cards. Your permanent departure to the Federal Republic of Germany will take place at 5 p.m. today, directly to Munich, for the purpose of reunion with your relatives there.
But we want to emigrate to West Berlin.

We packed everything we could carry and traveled on the train from Erfurt to East Berlin.

Is this seat free?

No one noticed that the soldier had hung his coat over my dad's jacket.

Inside the jacket were our denaturalization documents and identity cards—the only official papers we still had.

On April 6, 1984, we entered the crossing point at Bahnhof Friedrichstraße, commonly known as the Palace of Tears.

EINGANG
SEKTION A

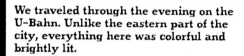

We traveled through the evening on the U-Bahn. Unlike the eastern part of the city, everything here was colorful and brightly lit.

We laughed and celebrated late into the night.

What's amazing is that even though I was so young, I can still clearly remember that night.

It's my first conscious memory.

The End

Glossary

Autobahn: the federal highway system of Germany

Bahnhof Friedrichstraße: a railway station in Berlin. During the Cold War, Bahnhof Friedrichstraße also served as a checkpoint between the different sections of Berlin.

Berlin Wall: a concrete divider between East Berlin and West Berlin, built by the DDR

Cold War: a conflict between the Soviet Union and the United States of America (as well as supporting nations) without direct military violence. The competing aims of communist nations and capitalist nations drove this conflict. The Cold War lasted from 1945 to 1991.

communism: a system (or the theory of a system) in which the members of a society collectively own goods and the means of production, as opposed to a system in which individuals own private property. *Communism* is also used to describe a system in which a state (led by one dominant political party) controls its own means of production.

Communist Manifesto, The: an 1848 publication by the influential economic and political writers Karl Marx and Friedrich Engels

compulsory: mandatory and often enforced by the threat of punishment

Deutsche Demokratische Republik (DDR): also known as the German Democratic Republic, or East Germany. Socialist political leaders controlled the DDR in the decades following World War II.

Deutsche Mark: a unit of currency in the Federal Republic of Germany

emigration: leaving one's home country for another place of residence

Free German Youth: also known as the *Freie Deutsche Jugend*, or the FDJ. The Free German Youth was an East German organization for young people, designed to promote socialist behavior and ideals.

Helsinki Accords: part of a 1975 conference designed to promote better relations among the communist and non-communist nations of Europe

Kommunistische Partei Deutschlands (KPD): also known as the Communist Party of Germany. This party was active in Germany from 1918 to 1933. In East Germany, the KPD became a part of the Socialist Unity Party of Germany at the start of the Cold War.

propaganda: information put forward to advance a particular group or cause. Propaganda often misleads readers, viewers, or listeners.

socialism: a system (or the theory of a system) of collective ownership and without private property. *Socialism* is sometimes used to describe all systems similar to communism and sometimes used to describe a system of partial communism.

Soviet Union: also known as the Union of Soviet Socialist Republics (USSR). The Soviet Union was a communist state that stretched across Europe and Asia, with leadership based in Moscow, Russia. It existed from 1922 until 1991.

Sozialistische Einheitspartei Deutschlands (SED): also known as the Socialist Unity Party of Germany. The SED was the governing political party of the Deutsche Demokratische Republik.

Stalinist: an approach or an attitude resembling the tactics of Joseph Stalin, leader of the Soviet Union from the mid-1920s until 1953. *Stalinist* is often used to describe communist policies (or similar policies) at their harshest and most oppressive.

Stasi: also known as the Ministerium für Staatssicherheit, or the Ministry for State Security. The Stasi were the state security service of the DDR. Stasi duties included spying on DDR citizens and fighting opposition to communist rule.

Winnetou: a fictional American Indian and the hero of a series of stories by German writer Karl May. May published many Winnetou adventures in the late nineteenth century and early twentieth century.

June 5, 1945: Following the surrender of German forces, the Allies of World War II divide Germany into four zones. Although the capital city of Berlin lies within the Soviet zone of occupation, the United States, Great Britain, France, and the Soviet Union each claim a section of the city, dividing Berlin into four zones as well.

June 1948: The United States, France, and Britain join their zones together under one currency. This area, West Berlin, enjoys greater economic success than communist-controlled East Berlin. As a result, many people living in East Berlin begin to move west. The Soviet Union attempts to block the Western powers' continued access to the city.

Late 1948: East Berlin and West Berlin establish separate governments. West Berlin is treated as an unofficial state of Germany's western region.

May 23, 1949: West Germany is formally established.

October 7, 1949: Berlin's Soviet zone declares itself an independent state: the Deutsche Demokratische Republik (also known as the DDR, or the German Democratic Republic). The Sozialistische Einheitspartei Deutschlands (also known as the SED, or the Socialist Unity Party) serves as the governing political party of this state.

June 16, 1953: Building workers in East Berlin's Stalinallee boulevard go on strike to protest increased work hours and withdrawn pay increases—a sign of growing frustration in the DDR. On June 17, Soviet troops intervene and use force to end the strikes. Many protesters are later executed after unjust legal proceedings.

August 13, 1961: Walter Ulbricht, chairman of the SED, grows concerned that East Berlin's economy will collapse if people from the area continue to seek refuge in the West. As a result, the police and the National People's Army of the DDR begin blocking off the eastern sector from the western sectors.

August 15, 1961: Workers start construction on a concrete wall between East Berlin and West Berlin. Eastern border guards are instructed to shoot anyone who attempts to escape.

December 17, 1963: Authorities in the DDR allow West Berliners to visit relatives in East Berlin over the winter holidays—but only between December 19 and January 5 and only with a permit. Before this date, the people of West Berlin were only allowed to visit certain sections of the city.

February 6, 1989: Border guards shoot and kill a young man trying to escape East Berlin. The man, Chris Gueffroy, becomes the final person to be shot while attempting to cross the border.

November 9, 1989: In response to protests, the DDR opens its borders to the Federal Republic of Germany—including West Berlin—allowing East German citizens to travel outside of the DDR.

November 10, 1989: Border guards of the DDR begin dismantling the Berlin Wall in order to create new crossing points. Citizens of both East Berlin and West Berlin join in the dismantling process. However, the Berlin Wall is not completely destroyed. Parts of the concrete wall are left as a memorial to those who died trying to cross it.

November 14, 1989: Ernst Höfner, finance minister of the DDR, reveals that the state's economic reports had been falsified and that the state had racked up a debt of 130 billion East German marks.

December 3, 1989: Members of the SED resign from office. Former party leader Erich Honecker is expelled from the party, along with other communist leaders.

October 3, 1990: Formal reunification of East and West Berlin is declared. The former DDR is incorporated into the Federal Republic of Germany. October 3 is now known as the Day of German Unity.

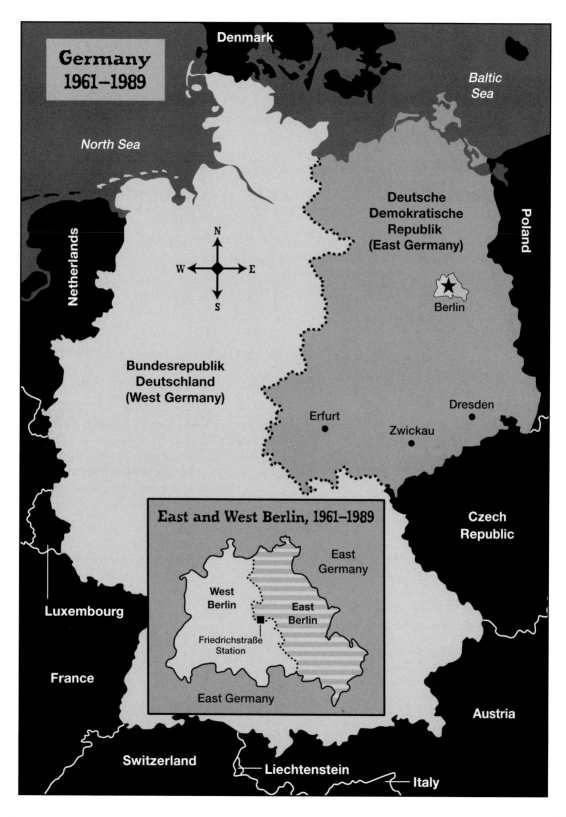

Germany
1961–1989

Denmark

Baltic Sea

North Sea

Deutsche
Demokratische
Republik
(East Germany)

Poland

N
W E
S

★
Berlin

Netherlands

Bundesrepublik
Deutschland
(West Germany)

Dresden

Erfurt

Zwickau

Czech
Republic

East and West Berlin, 1961–1989

West
Berlin

East
Germany

East
Berlin

Friedrichstraße
Station

Luxembourg

East Germany

France

Austria

Switzerland

Liechtenstein

Italy

Simon Schwartz was born in Erfurt in 1982 and grew up in the Kreuzberg neighborhood of Berlin. In 2004, he relocated to Hamburg to study illustration at the Hamburg University of Applied Sciences. Five years later, he had completed his debut graphic novel, *drüben!* It is available in the United States as *The Other Side of the Wall.* In 2010, the book won the ICOM Independent Comic Prize in the Outstanding Scenario category and was nominated for the German Youth Literature Prize. In 2012, his second graphic novel, *Packeis,* won the Max-und-Moritz Prize for Best German Comic. That year he also contributed artwork to a memorial and education center located in the former Stasi headquarters of Erfurt. His drawing—printed on glass plates, measuring seven meters by forty meters, and forming a cube around the building—is Germany's largest memorial for victims of Stasi terror. In 2013, he was awarded the Hans Meid prize for German graphic art.

Simon Schwartz's comics and illustrations are published regularly in various newspapers and magazines, including *Frankfurter Allgemeine Sonntagszeitung, Der Freitag, GEOlino* and *Die Zeit.* He currently teaches illustration at the Hamburg University of Applied Sciences. More of his work is viewable online at www.simon-schwartz.com.